LEE'S 3 HABITS

A Handbook
for Stronger Relationships
and Greater Happiness

Written by
Dr. Paul L. Corona

Artwork by
Eddie Rosas

Lee's 3 Habits:
A Handbook for Stronger Relationships and Greater Happiness

Written by Dr. Paul L. Corona
Artwork by Eddie Rosas

ISBN: 978-1-79033-686-9

For anyone who would like to be a little happier.

CONTENTS

FOREWORD

Stronger relationships make us happier. It doesn't matter who we are, where we're from, or what we do for a living. I know this from my 70 years of life experience, including over 35 years coaching more than 150 CEOs and their management teams around the world. Decades of scholarly research suggest the same thing – close relationships are one of the strongest and most important predictors of happiness.

All of us can *build* stronger relationships by doing a better job of three things we already do every day: asking, listening and giving. Unfortunately, this isn't easy. It goes against our natural tendencies. When interacting with others, most of us *tell* more than we *ask*, we *talk* more than we *listen*, and we *take* more than we *give* – without even realizing it.

One of life's irrefutable laws is . . . stronger relationships and greater happiness take work. That's why I'm so excited about the ***Lee's 3 Habits*** system that Paul Corona and Eddie Rosas created to help us actually *do* the work. It's short, it's simple, and . . . *it works*!

Dr. Marshall Goldsmith
New York Times and *Wall Street Journal* #1 bestselling author
World's top leadership coach (*Fast Company*, *Global Gurus*, *Inc.*)
Thinkers50 Hall of Fame inductee

CREATORS

Written by . . .

Dr. Paul L. Corona is a clinical professor of leadership in the Kellogg School of Management at Northwestern University, where his teaching and coaching ratings average 95/100. Paul is also the founder of the ***Lee's 3 Habits*** system, which helps motivated people build stronger relationships and achieve greater happiness, and the author of *The Wisdom of Walk-Ons: 7 Winning Strategies for College, Business and Life.* Paul is a certified leadership coach and a Marshall Goldsmith "100 Coaches" honoree, selected from more than 16,000 candidates to advance the practice of coaching with Dr. Goldsmith, who is recognized as the world's top leadership coach. During the past 33 years, Paul has transformed himself from a business person into a performance improvement specialist. He previously held a variety of leadership roles in Fortune 500 corporations, a Big 4 accounting and consulting firm, and major research universities. Most importantly, Paul is a husband, parent and friend.

Artwork by . . .

Eddie Rosas, a two-time Emmy nominated filmmaker, has worked in the animation industry for over 25 years. He's a director for Glen Keane Productions at Netflix Animation in Hollywood. Earlier in his career, Eddie had the pleasure of working on the highly acclaimed animated productions *The Simpsons* (for 16 seasons), *Futurama* and *The Iron Giant*. Originally from Alaska, Eddie is a graduate of the Walt Disney founded school, California Institute of the Arts. When he's not bringing characters to life at work, Eddie can be found teaching the *Storyboarding* course at Woodbury University in Burbank, where he's been an adjunct professor since 2002.

INTRODUCTION

Let's be honest, most of us would like to be a little happier. It's a natural human desire. Unfortunately, it's also natural for us to do things that actually decrease our happiness. When interacting with others we tend to tell, talk and take too much. Telling, talking and taking don't make us happier – asking, listening and giving do. *Ask*, *listen* and *give*. These three simple habits strengthen our relationships with others, and stronger relationships (not more fame, fortune or achievement) are the real keys to greater happiness.

The ***Lee's 3 Habits*** system helps motivated people build stronger relationships and achieve greater happiness:

- Start by watching the 3-minute micro-movie about Lee's transformation.
- Then read this 30-minute handbook.

- For a guided learning experience, schedule a 90-minute workshop for your group.

All of this is available at www.lees3habits.com.

1. OUR HAPPINESS LEVELS

Do you think most people would like to be a little happier with their lives?

Over 90% of the people I ask say, "Yes."

On a rating scale of 1-10, with 10 being the highest, how happy are *you* with *your* life? How high would you like to go?

I'm at 8, overall, and on any given day I can jump to 9 or 10 . . . or drop to 7, 6, 5 or even 4. My goal is to consistently hit 9.

If you'd like to consistently hit a higher number, this handbook (and the ***Lee's 3 Habits*** system) will help.

2. COMPELLING RESEARCH

For over 2,000 years, humans have attempted to achieve true happiness. Early on, ancient philosophers, theologians and artists did their best to help. Eventually, modern psychologists, self-help authors and life coaches joined the mix and started a happiness movement. Almost all of these helpers have had great intentions, but they've also (unintentionally) overwhelmed most of us. Frankly, we now have too many ideas, frameworks and tools that sound good (and *are* good) but don't actually get used enough. So the current happiness movement, for many people, has become one big failed New Year's resolution. I believe this is a significant problem.

One way to solve a complex problem is to keep the solution simple. That's what Albert Einstein suggested in 1922, at the Imperial Hotel in Tokyo, after winning the Nobel Prize in Physics. Instead of tipping a messenger with money, Einstein wrote him two notes about how to live a happier life:

- "A calm and modest life brings more happiness than the pursuit of success combined with constant restlessness."

- "Where there's a will there's a way."

In 2017, these two simple notes sold at auction for $1.56 million!

Einstein's advice sounds wise, and it can serve as a foundation for happy living, but we should also consider what "happiness researchers" have discovered.

Oxford, one of the world's most respected universities, is home to the world's largest university press. In 2014, they published *The Oxford Handbook of Happiness*, a 1,097-page discussion of what the world's psychologists know about how to achieve true happiness. Here are three highlights:

1. The subject of happiness ". . . consumed Socrates, Plato and Aristotle . . ." over 2,000 years ago.

2. "Social relationships have long been considered one of the strongest and most important predictors of happiness."

3. ". . . decades of theoretical and empirical work highlight that being in a close relationship, the number of close relationships one has, and the quality of relationship experiences in general, are robust and consistent correlates of happiness . . . across cultures."

In 2015, a team of researchers at Harvard University shared findings from their *Harvard Study of Adult Development*, the longest running examination (in history) of what makes people healthy and happy. Here are three highlights:

1. True happiness is not about fame, fortune or high-achievement.

2. Good relationships keep us happier, healthier and living longer. They can be formed with family, friends and community. It's about quality, not quantity.

3. Relationships are not always smooth. We need to be able to count on each other when times get tough. There are no quick fixes. It's messy and complicated. It takes hard work . . . and the work never ends.

In 2017, an additional team of university researchers published findings from their brain-scanning study of how social connections influence our thoughts and feelings (in the *Proceedings of the National Academy of Sciences of the United States of America*, one of the world's most respected scholarly journals). Here are three highlights:

1. "Humans are fundamentally motivated to connect with others, spending considerable time and energy investing in social relationships."
2. "A lack of social connection resulting from social isolation has a significant negative impact on health and well-being."
3. They cited related research published in *Science* (2003), which suggests social rejection and physical pain produce similar brain responses. They both make us feel extraordinary stress,

which we then have to get under control in order to feel good again.

This is why it can hurt so much to be ignored on the playground, excluded from a party, or broken up with by our life partner.

The bottom line is . . . relationships influence our happiness, a lot.

3. SO WHAT SHOULD WE DO?

A key question is . . . if stronger relationships make us happier, then how can we build them?

The best answer I know is . . . by focusing less on ourselves and more on others.

Of course this strategy is simple, but it's not easy. One of life's irrefutable laws is . . . stronger relationships (and greater happiness) don't come effortlessly, they take hard work.

The good news is . . . all of us can *build* stronger relationships by doing a better job of three things we already do every day: *asking*, *listening* and *giving*. Unfortunately, this isn't easy because it goes against our natural tendencies. When interacting with others, most of us *tell* more than we *ask*, we *talk* more than we *listen*, and we *take* more than we *give* – without even realizing it.

That's what often happens to our friend Lee. He's *naturally* and *unconsciously* focused on himself most of the time. He *tells*, *talks* and *takes* too much. Lee doesn't mean to *offend* people, but he does. Then his relationships suffer, and everyone's unhappy as a result.

For example, when Lee is too focused on himself during a conversation, he tends to:

- *Tell* . . . by saying something like, "*I* know the answer!"

- *Talk* . . . by saying something like, "Here's what happened to *me*."

- *Take* . . . by thinking something like, "What's in it for *me*?"

On the other hand, whenever Lee *intentionally* focuses more on others, he becomes a better version of himself. By *asking*, *listening* and *giving* more, Lee *engages* people. Then his relationships get stronger, and everyone's happier as a result.

For example, when Lee is more focused on others during a conversation, he tends to:

- *Ask* . . . by saying something like, "What do *you* think?"

- *Listen* . . . by saying something like, "Are you saying [*his understanding of what they're saying*]?"

- *Give* . . . by thinking and saying something like, "How can I *help*?"

The bottom line for Lee (and all of us) is . . . it's all about staying balanced, meaning we need to:

- *Tell* less and *ask* more.

- *Talk* less and *listen* more.

- *Take* less and *give* more.

Now let's define ***Lee's 3 Habits*** with some specific examples. Then let's think of a few ways *we* can do a better job of *asking*, *listening* and *giving* in our own lives.

4. HABIT #1: ASK

Ask insightful questions with a *genuine interest* in learning about other people, *their* ideas and *their* experiences. (Please don't just tell them about yourself, *your* ideas and *your* experiences.)

Here are some good examples of insightful questions:

- What do you think about [topic]?
- What do you like to do [for fun / at work]?
- What's going especially well for you?
- What's one thing you'd like to do better?
- How can I help?

Please write a few specific ideas of how *you* can do a better job of asking:

5. HABIT #2: LISTEN

Listen patiently and closely to *understand* what other people are really saying. (Please don't *pretend* to listen politely while you're actually waiting for an opportunity to jump in and say something smart, funny or interesting.)

Here are some good ways to listen patiently and closely:

- Ask insightful questions.
- Give undivided attention (don't multitask).
- Use respectful non-verbal language (eye contact, body posture, facial expressions).
- Let them finish talking (don't interrupt).
- Repeat back your understanding of what they said.

Please write a few specific ideas of how *you* can do a better job of listening:

6. HABIT #3: GIVE

Give generously to *help* other people move forward or feel better. (Please don't treat them like instruments for getting what *we* want, with an attitude that says, "What's in it for *me*?")

Here are some good ways to give generously:

- Respect . . . by listening patiently and closely
- Assistance . . . by providing services
- Suggestions . . . by offering ideas
- Solutions . . . by supplying answers
- Appreciation . . . by expressing thanks

Please write a few specific ideas of how *you* can do a better job of giving:

LEE'S 3 HABITS

7. MOVING FORWARD AND STAYING ON TRACK

One of life's irrefutable laws is . . . stronger relationships and greater happiness take work. So if we're fortunate enough to be physically, intellectually and emotionally healthy – and we do all the work that's required to form ***Lee's 3 Habits*** – then we *will* build stronger relationships, and we *will* achieve greater happiness. We first need to embrace the unavoidable, three-step challenge:

- Step 1 – Be humble: "I *need* to get better."
- Step 2 – Have desire: "I *want* to get better."
- Step 3 – Stay disciplined: "I will *do* all the work."

Many people are humble and have desire, but few of us stay disciplined over time. Why? Almost all of us begin with good intentions. We really do want to get better. So we get off to a fast start, and then . . . we stop . . . for all kinds of valid reasons we *imperfect human beings* create for ourselves: we're too busy, we're too tired, we forget . . . the list goes on and on.

So here's the best way I know for moving forward and staying on track. It's a simple process for changing our behaviors (from too much *telling*, *talking* and *taking* to more *asking*, *listening* and *giving*). If we just stick with the process, then our asking, listening and giving *behaviors* will eventually become *habits*: ***Lee's 3 Habits***!

The *Lee's 3 Habits* process

Post the words **ASK – LISTEN – GIVE** somewhere in your home, at work, and in your calendar. Then:

1. Read the words **ASK – LISTEN – GIVE** once when you wake up in the morning, once during the day, and once before bed at night. (All of this should take a total of one minute.)

2. Rate (on a scale of 1-10) how well you did that day – with your *asking*, *listening* and *giving* – in a habit-tracking app, a journal, or any other tool that works for you. (All of this should take a total of one minute.)

3. Talk with a committed support partner – once a week – about what you both *did well* that week and can *do better* the next week. (All of this should take a total of 10 minutes / 5 minutes per person.)

8. ONE PERSON AND ONE E-MAIL

If you're committed to building stronger relationships and achieving greater happiness with ***Lee's 3 Habits***, the best thing you can do is start right now. Here are two essential actions you can take to ensure success:

1. Think of one person with whom you'd like to do more *asking*, *listening* and *giving* – and get started with them right away. It could be someone who's especially important to you, someone who's giving you a problem, or someone fun.

2. Send me an e-mail (plcorona@lees3habits.com) – 30 days from today (please put a reminder in your calendar) – and let me know how you're doing with ***Lee's 3 Habits***:

    - What results are you seeing?

    - What questions or comments do you have?

9. GROUP WORKSHOPS

The ***Lee's 3 Habits*** system helps motivated people build stronger relationships and achieve greater happiness:

- Start by watching the 3-minute micro-movie about Lee's transformation.
- Then read this 30-minute handbook.
- **For a guided learning experience, schedule a 90-minute workshop for your group by e-mailing plcorona@lees3habits.com or calling 630-297-5120.**

All of this is available at www.lees3habits.com.

ACKNOWLEDGEMENTS

The ***Lee's 3 Habits*** system took 55 years to create. It reflects everything I've learned from countless family members, friends, teachers, classmates, coaches, teammates, mentors, colleagues and clients with whom I've been extremely fortunate to live and work. I wish I could thank all of you by name. I'm especially indebted to my . . .

- ***Lee's 3 Habits*** partner, Eddie Rosas, whose magical artwork and animation give Lee and his friends life

- *Lee's Transformation* movie stars – Lance Bennett, Elizabeth Corona and Brenda Knapp – who give Lee and his friends perfectly relatable personalities

- Sound experts – Colin Sipos, Adam Wiebe and Tom Wiebe of Earhole Studios in Chicago, Illinois

USA – for making the ***Lee's 3 Habits*** system an impeccable sensory experience

- Editor, Lesley Kagan Wynes, whose expertise and insight I appreciate almost as much as our friendship

- Father, Richard Corona, who taught me how and why to work hard

- Guru, Marshall Goldsmith, who teaches us how to coach for results and pay it forward

- Role model, Harry Kraemer, who shows us what it means to be a world-class CEO and an even better person

- Adviser, Carter Cast, who helps me grow – professionally and personally – and makes me laugh

- Guide, Bernie Banks, who gives me unmatched opportunity, support and inspiration

- Best friend, Jen Jacobus Corona, who is also the best life partner I could ever have

- Daughters, Elizabeth and Margaret Corona, who give me indescribable joy and a reason to love unconditionally

Dr. Paul L. Corona
Optimus Coaching LLC
Chicago, Illinois USA

BIBLIOGRAPHY

Bilefsky, Dan (October 25, 2017) "Albert Einstein's 'Theory of Happiness' Fetches $1.56 Million" *The New York Times*

David, Susan A.; Boniwell Ilona; Conley Ayers, Amanda – editors – (2014) *The Oxford Handbook of Happiness*

Eisenberger, Naomi I.; Lieberman, Matthew D.; Williams, Kipling D. (October 10, 2003) "Does rejection hurt? An fMRI study of social exclusion" *Science*

Lieberman, Matthew D.; Jarcho, Johanna M.; Berman, Steve; Naliboff, Bruce D.; Suyenobu, Brandall Y.; Mandelkern, Mark; Mayer, Emeran A. (May 2004) "The neural correlates of placebo effects: a disruption account" *NeuroImage*

Rock, David (August 27, 2009) "Managing with the brain in mind: Neuroscience research is revealing the social nature of the high-performance workplace" *strategy+business*

Schmälzle, Ralf; O'Donnell, Matthew Brook; Garcia, Javier O.; Cascio, Christopher N.; Bayer, Joseph; Bassett, Danielle S.; Vettel, Jean M.; Falk, Emily B. (May 16, 2017) "Brain connectivity dynamics during social interaction reflect social network structure" *Proceedings of the National Academy of Sciences of the United States of America*

Waldinger, Robert (2015) "What makes a good life? Lessons from the longest study on happiness" *TEDxBeaconStreet*

Made in the USA
Columbia, SC
18 March 2021

34298115R00024